Mix

The Civil War in Randolph County, Missouri

By Berry Lee Canote

Cover Photo: General Oden Guitar, Commander of the 9th Cavalry Missouri State Militia

Published by Berry Lee Canote
2017

Table of Contents

Foreword: Prelude to War

The 1884 and 1920 histories of Randolph County do not cover the American Civil War in any depth. With the 1884 history it could be argued the war was too recent. There were many men who had fought in the war who would still have hard feelings about things that had happened. The person who lived across the road may well have been on the other side. Therefore, the 1884 histories may have avoided the issue of the War so as to spare the sensitivities of men and women that were still relatively young when the war took place.

As for the 1920 history of the county, it is anyone's guess as to why the Civil War was not covered in any great detail. It certainly was not lack of information as the official reports were even then ready at hand. Nor can it be argued that the war had been deemed unimportant. Numerous news stories had appeared in the years after the war about raids and battles.

It is hoped this book can somewhat remedy the shortcomings of the previous histories. Sadly, there is much we will never know about events of the American Civil War in Randolph County, Missouri. The information simply was not recorded, or was only noted in a brief news story in a newspaper. In some cases the accounts of recent events found in Civil War era newspapers may be inaccurate. The number of the enemy in an action may have been exaggerated to make the opposing units seem more heroic, or there simply was no reliable way to get an accurate count of the units involved. Where there are no official reports, who was in command of the units is questionable. This can be seen in differences between newspaper accounts and the official reports.

Reading issues of the newspaper the *Randolph Citizen* (which was based in Huntsville in the late 1850s and off and on throughout the 1860s), it was clear to the citizens of the county that the events of 1860 were going to lead to war. What concerned them was the election, events on the Kansas and Missouri border, as well as state politics. Looking over issues of the *Citizen* one will notice that for Randolph County the issue of secession was a complex one. This was only natural. The county had been settled in the 1820s by people from the Carolinas, Kentucky, Tennessee, and Virginia. Many of these settlers were slaveholders, and brought their slaves with them. Here the slaves were used to raise hemp and tobacco, the two big cash crops of this region of Missouri. The culture of the county therefore was that of the Upper South. However, it was with a Western outlook. Frontier life was still a recent memory, and at that time Missouri was on the western edge of the states of the United States. In the late 1850s, the county also desired many of the benefits of the industrial North such as railroads and textile industries. Coal was just beginning to be mined as well. Finally, an influx of German immigrants also changed the character of the county. The identity of the county was therefore in flux at the end of the 1850s. It no longer was an agrarian society like that of the Upper South, and had much in common with the West with a desire to have the amenities of the North.

It is no surprise then that loyalties within the county were divided. Some wished to go the way the South would go. Others desired to remain with the Union. Some of the Union men were slaveholders that could not see a nation without slavery. Others who were pro-South had never owned slaves. The issue of allegiances in Randolph County was a complex one with each man and woman determining their loyalties based on their own personal views. So while Randolph County was a part of the slave holding region known as Little Dixie there was no guarantee that the county would go with the South in 1860.

According to the September 13, 1860 edition of the *Randolph Citizen*, there was a, "Mass Meeting" of the Democratic Party in Huntsville on September 10th. Doctor William Fort was elected President. Doctor Walker and Robert Mitchell were elected Vice Presidents, and James D. Head Secretary. A committee of seven was appointed to prepare resolutions. The men on this committee were W. A. Hall, George M. Quinn, William McCann, J. S. Harlan, Doctor J. T. Fort, W. I. Ferguson, and J. B. Dameron. While the committee was meeting, C. F. Jackson and J. B. Clark addressed the meeting. At the meeting the following resolutions were unanimously adopted:

Resolved, That the preservation of this Union is of far more importance to us than any of the questions supposed to be at issue in the pending Presidential contest. That existence will be greatly endangered by the success of the Black Republican party, and that the only hope of its defeat is by the Democratic party in the Free States; therefore

Resolved, That the Democratic party of the Free States are entitled to our warmest sympathies in their efforts in the present contest that any efforts to diminish their

*strength, meets with our decided condemnation, and
that having expressed their preference for Stephen A.
Douglas for the Presidency, we hold it a duty to unite
with them in securing his election.*

*Resolved, That we have undiminished confidence in
our public servants, C. F. Jackson and Jno. B. Clark,
and that in using their efforts to unite the Democratic
party on the only man who can defeat the enemies of
our Union, they have an additional claim to our
confidence.*

*Resolved, That the proceedings of this meeting be
published in the Missouri Republican, Howard county
Banner, and Randolph Citizen. WM FORT, Pres't. Jas.
P. Head, Sec'y.*

At this point, there were no calls for secession in the
county. The main concern was the defeat of the
Republican Party in the Presidential election. And
going by this single meeting, the majority of the
leading men of the county supported that aim. In the
May 2, 1861 edition of the *Citizen,* Judge Hall spoke
strongly against secession in a letter to the editor, and
the war that would result, and in the January 1, 1861
edition of the *Citizen* a letter to the editor signed
simply "Toulman of Randolph" strongly advocated
secession. Then in the April 25, 1861 edition of the

Citizen the following story on a meeting held on April 20th appeared:

Pursuant to a previous notice, a respectable portion of the citizens of Randolph county, Mo., met at Oak Grove Academy on Saturday, April '20th, 1861, at which the following proceedings were had : On motion of Dr. Win. McLean, H. Stamper was called to the chair, and James Bradley appointed Secretary. The Chair briefly stated the object of the meeting, and in pursuance of a previous motion appointed the following named gentlemen as a committee to draft resolutions expressive of the sense of the meeting: Dr. Win. B McLean, James Bradley, Wm. Cobb, Dr. P. C. Yates, Robert Gayle. The Committee after a short absence reported the following resolutions, which were unanimously adopted. Whereas, With painful regret we have seen the proclamation of President Lincoln, calling on the states of this Union for troops avowedly for the purpose of putting down combinations against the enforcement of the laws, and to "protect the public propor y; put, as we Believe, for the wicked and atrocious object of submitting our brethren of the South, therefore be it Resolved bv this meeting. 1st. That President Lincoln in his proclamation has shown a disregard of Constitutional law equaled only by his atrocious recklessness for the lives of the people. 2d. That we cordially approve the course of Governor

6

Jackson in promptly refusing to furnish troops as demanded of Missouri. 3d. That we are in favor of changing the relationship of Missouri to the General Government as soon as the same can be affected, 4th. That we ask the members of this conventional district to support the views above indicated. 5th. That without regard to those differences of opinions that may have heretofore divided us as to the course pursued by the seceded States, we declare our purpose indissoluble to connect our destiny with theirs, whatsoever may take us. That the citizens of Randolph County who are willing to endorse the above Resolutions meet in Huntsville on Saturday, the 4th day of May next. James Bradley then offered the following, which was, without a dissenting voice, adopted : Resolved, That this meeting appoint a committee of seven to inquire of Representatives from this decided to the State Convention their position in the present contest, and that said committee be requited to report to the convention at Huntsville on Saturday, May the 4th, 1861: In accordance therewith the following were appointed said committee : Dr. Wm. B. McLean, James Bradley, H. T. Fort, Augustine Bradsher, Robert Gayle, A. M. Bradsher, Wm. Cobb. It was then resolved that a copy of the proceedings be sent to the ' - Randolph Citizen" for publication. On motion the meeting adjourned. H. STAMPER, Chairman. James Bradley, Sec'y.

As seen from the above stories in the *Randolph Citizen*, the county was divided between pro-Southern and pro-Northern forces. This division seemed to go along social classes and urban vs. rural. The wealthy men of Huntsville tended to be pro-Northern, while both the wealthy and poor of the rural areas tended to be pro-Southern. While this is a generalization, it nonetheless holds true. It is no wonder then with its mixed allegiances that Randolph County would be a hotbed of activity during the Civil War even if none of it was major.

Despite nothing major going on, there were a lot of smaller events that would take place, some of which would impact other areas. Within the county, arrests, forced conscriptions, robberies, vandalism of railroad property would take place weekly. At that time, Huntsville was still the center of a major north-south stage road, as well as an east-west one. In addition, the North Missouri Railroad ran through the eastern part of the county, and was a target for guerillas seeking to disrupt Union communications and supply lines. Randolph County therefore saw a lot of troop movements which meant several skirmishes took place as well as one minor battle.

And as stated above, there is a lot of information that has been lost. An example of this is the April 1, 1864 raid by guerilla Bill Stephens on Cairo, Missouri. All that is known is the raid took place. No other details are known. Beyond Bill Stephens, it is not who else was involved, whether anyone was shot, or what stores, if any were robbed. Similarly, the location of a skirmish on September 20, 1863 is not known beyond taking place somewhere in Randolph County. Luckily, other details of the skirmish such as names of the commanders, and number of men are known. Finally, a raid on Renick by guerilla Thomas Hunter that took place on September 10, 1863 lacks adequate documentation. All that is known is that Hunter had about ten men, and robbed two stores. How many more incidents went unrecorded is anyone's guess. Hopefully, with time and more research more information will be uncovered.

Today, many are only vaguely aware of events in Randolph County during the war. They know "Bloody Bill" Anderson hailed from Huntsville. More may know that Anderson even raided Huntsville. That though may be the extent of their knowledge concerning the war in Randolph County. It is hoped that this book can enlighten the reader on many of the events that took place in the county. It does not cover everything. There were many arrests made, some that ended in jail time that are not mentioned here. These are too numerous to contain in such a small volume. There were also several murders and robberies that did not have much impact on the war. Again, as with the arrests, they are not mentioned here. What is contained in this book are most all the skirmishes that took place as well as many of the other major incidents within the county. Where possible, primary sources such as official reports or newspaper accounts are quoted.

Chapter One: 1861

The early stages of the war were uneventful in Randolph County. Most of the time was spent by Confederate commanders recruiting for General Sterling Price's army. Troops that were recruited did not remain in the county, but were sent away to other parts of Missouri. Similarly, Union recruits were sent to other parts of the state or even the nation. Randolph County was not of strategic importance to the war effort. While Huntsville was an important town at the time, it paled in comparison to such targets as Boonville. The first major action to take place in the county was Poindexter's train robbery at Old Allen.

August 28, 1861: Colonel John Poindexter's Train Robbery

In what is often thought to be the first daylight train robbery in the United States, Colonel John Poindexter and Confederate regulars seized gold and securities of the Bank of the State of Missouri. Knowing that the monies were being shipped out of state, Poindexter stopped the train being used to ship the gold and securities on the North Missouri Railroad at Allen, near the present town of Moberly, Missouri. Reportedly, three trunks containing $100,000 were seized, and then returned to the bank in Fayette, Missouri. A news story on the action appeared in the August 30th, 1861 edition of the *Saint Louis Daily Missouri Republican* and is as follows:

Seizure of Funds Belonging to the Fayette Branch of the State Bank, by the State Troops

We learn from passengers on the North Missouri Railroad, in last night, that a committee of gentlemen left Fayette, on Wednesday last, with $100,00 in coin belonging to the Branch Bank of that place, for removal to New York. At Allen, the railroad station, a company of armed men, headed by Capt. POINDEXTER, of General Price's army, took it in possession, and removed it to their camp, some eight miles north.

Prompt efforts were made by the committee and other citizens of Fayette to recover it, and at our latest advice Capt. POINDEXTER was marching in the direction of the Bank with the money; some saying he was attempting to cross the river and reach Gen. PRICE's army, and others that he had been induced to return the money to the Bank.

In the opinion of the informant who received his information from gentlemen of Fayette, that the money would go to the Bank, but nothing is certainly known on the subject.

December 21, 1861: Attack on Guerillas Destroying Tracks of North Missouri Railroad

The location of these incidents are known only as being along the North Missouri Railroad in the vicinity of Renick and Allen. Lt. Col. Erastus Morse with a dozen horsemen surprised 150 guerrillas destroying the tracks of the North Missouri Railroad near Renick, and drove them off. After waiting for 70 men of Birge's Western Sharpshooters, they pushed their train to Allen where they surprised another group of men destroying tracks. Lt. Col. Morse was wounded having been shot in the thigh.

He and his men then returned to Renick where they were joined by 45 men from the 10th Missouri Infantry under Capt. William Forbes, and another 50 men from Col. William Bishop's Black Hawk Cavalry. The next day they surprised a band of 300 near Sturgeon. Lt. Col. Morse died January 3, 1852 from the wounds he received near Allen in the incident (*Saint Louis Daily Missouri Republican* January 3rd, 1862 edition). It could well be the number of the rebel forces are exaggerated. That fourteen men could surprise and drive off 150 seems a bit far-fetched.

13

A portion of a letter to the editor, signed only with, "M" in the *Daily Missouri Republican* describes the actions as follows:

Between Sturgeon and Renick, the alarm was given that we had run upon a band bout to destroy the road. The cars were stopped, the rebels chased off and their tools captured. We soon started on, not dreaming of the work beyond. Three miles north of Renick we were stopped by the destruction of the road by fire, a hundred yards or more had been torn up, and large quantities of wood piled on the track and the ties destroyed. Here the Colonel and twelve or fourteen of our men left the cars in haste and dashed ahead in search of the enemy, while the cars were sent back to bring up a reinforcement of Col. BIRGE's Sharp Shooters, five companies of which were stationed at Renick. Our small force of fourteen found the rebels, one hundred and fifty strong, on the north of the fire, where a heavy stock train of twenty or twenty five cars had been stopped, and which they were preparing to burn, having captured the owners and drivers. The enemy fled the wildest confusion before the rush of our gallant boys, releasing their prisoners, every one seeking only his own safety. After the first onslaught our men divided and secreting themselves captured two of the burners, who seeing everything quiet, returned to note the progress of the fire. A third one escaped, but left behind bloody tokens that our powder and lead had not been spent in vain. In the morning, we pushed on to Allen, the next station; our boys mounted, and the Sharp Shooters, about seventy in number, in the cars. As the cars ran slowly, our boys reached Allen in advance, and found the rebels had been busy in the same demonic work of destruction. Colonel MORSE, at the head of the troop, charged upon the retreating rebels, and in pursuing one, received three buckshot through the left thigh beside several other marks of his person (Saint Louis Daily Missouri Republican, December 31st, 1861 edition)

Chapter Two: 1862

While in the Eastern Theater of the War things were in full swing, in Randolph County things were just getting started. The year began with a battle, the first and only one fought within the county's borders. This battle put a damper on Confederate operations within the county, and made for a fairly uneventful year for military operations.

January 7, 1862: Battle of Roan's Tan Yard Also Known as the Battle of Silver Creek

1861 was a time of heavy recruiting for the Confederate Army in Randolph County. Col. John A. Poindexter and Col. Joseph C. Porter were recruiting units in the county, and this did not include other companies raised by men such as Captain James Matlock. It was therefore vital to the Union Army that these efforts be stopped. It was on January 7, 1862 that Union forces moved against a Confederate camp commanded by Col. Poindexter on Silver Creek on the land of Joel Smith not far from the present town of Higbee in an effort to put an end to Confederate recruiting in Randolph County.

Rumors of a Confederate force in Randolph County had been going round for about a week. Poindexter's force was located the morning of January 7th, 1862. Detachments from the 1st and 2nd Missouri Cavalry, 4th Ohio Cavalry, and 1st Iowa Cavalry of the Union Army commanded by Maj. W.M.G. Torrence moved northeast from Howard County that day.

They reached the camp in the late afternoon, and despite heavy fog the Union forces numbering 450 attacked the 800 Confederates camped there. The battle was a complete rout lasting only about forty minutes. The Confederates were ill equipped and were largely untrained raw recruits, and not prepared to face well trained military units. This Union victory largely ended Confederate recruiting in Randolph County, and postponed most combat in the county until the summer of 1864. The official reports are as follows:

On January 7, 1862 information came that Col. J.A. Poindexter and a Confederate force were camped on Silver Creek in Randolph County. Detachments from the 1st and 2nd Missouri Cavalry, 4th Ohio Cavalry, and 1st Iowa Cavalry led by Maj. W.M.G. Torrence, all and all, numbering about 450 men proceeded to Silver Creek from Fayette. Upon arriving at Silver Creek the Union forces attacked the camp, and routed the Confederate force. After the battle they destroyed

17

the camp. The Union forces lost 6 men while the Confederates lost 40

Captain J. B. Watson, of the rebel army (and believed to have been concerned in the Magi burning), now on recruiting service near here, was captured, with two of his men, to-day by a part of my command.

I have the honor to be, sir, very respectfully, your obedient servant,

LEWIS MERRILL,
Colonel, Commanding Merrill's Horse.

Captain J. C. KELTON,
Assistant Adjutant-General.

HEADQUARTERS MERRILL'S HORSE,

Columbia, Mo., January 10, 1862.

CAPTAIN: I have the honor to report that on the night of Sunday, the 5th, nearly at daylight, I received a dispatch from Colonel Birge (at Sturgeon), stating that a part of some 300 or 400 rebels had camped that night at Renick, and were to move next morning to Roanoke, some 12 or 15 miles from there, with the object of crossing the river at Arrow Rock or Brunswick, and stating that he would attempt to overtake them by daylight of the 6th, and requesting me to co-operate. Not approving the plan proposed for me by Colonel Birge, I sent Lieutenant-Colonel Shaffer, with all the men I could spare, to go by way of Fayette and thence north towards Roanoke and cut off the retreat of the enemy, should Colonel Birge's command not success in overtaking him at Renick. Colonel Birge, I understand, went to Renick, and not finding the enemy, returned to Sturgeon the same day. Lieutenant-Colonel Shaffer reached Fayette late the night of the 6th, and there found a large cavalry force, consisting of detachments from the First Missouri Cavalry, under command of Major Hubbard, First Iowa Cavalry, under Major Torrence, and Merrill's Horse, under Major Hunt. He then learned during the night that the enemy, variously estimated at from 1,300 to 2,500, were encamped on Smith's farm, about 5 miles from Roanoke. At the same time he received information that the remains of the command of Colonel Dorsey, which had been engaged in the Mount Zion fight, was then marching to attack me at Columbia. I had only part of one company left when Colonel Shaffer City to escort the provision train. Early next morning he sent the command of Major Hubbard, which he had found at Fayette, re-enforced by one company of his own command, to find the enemy's camp, and returned at once to Columbia with the rest of his command.

Major Hubbard found the enemy's camp about 14 miles northwest of Fayette about 3 o'clock p. m., and immediately attacked them, routing them completely and taking possession of their camp, which he entirely destroyed. I have no official reports of the engagement form the part of my regiment engaged, and I presume before this Major Hubbard's reports have been received. The loss of my regiment was 2 killed and 3 wounded. The enemy's loss is not positively reported, but 5 are known to have been killed and 14 taken prisoners. This is only what is certainly known.

August 4, 1862: Occupation of Huntsville by Col. John Poindexter

The Battle of Roan's Tan Yard was so decisive that the Spring and Summer of 1862 were largely quiet in the county. Despite this Col. Poindexter managed to raise a sizeable force of men and entered the town of Huntsville on August 4th. The Union Army had largely left the town ungarrisoned thus allowing this to happen. Col. Poindexter occupied Huntsville with 700 to 800 men. He told the residents he was there "to put down armed forces and rebellion against the rights of the citizens of Missouri." He further said he would not interfere with the rights of Union men in any way, but would protect their persons and property, unless they

be found in arms. He then left the town in the direction
of Keytesville, probably taking what is now Route C to
Route O west of Huntsville which was the old stage
road. What prompted him to leave town is unknown.
(*Macon Gazette,* August 4, 1862 edition).

September 8, 1862: Attack on a Guerillas' Camp by Merrill's Horse

Captain J.W. Baird and members of Merrill's Horse
and the Enrolled Militia attacked a guerilla camp near
Roanoke. In the fight Captain Baird was killed, but
otherwise there were no Union losses. Four guerillas
were killed, one was wounded, and three were taken
prisoner. The names of the guerillas, not even their
commander are known. Below is a notice of Baird's
death in the September 15th, 1862 of the *Saint Louis
Daily Missouri Republican:*

CAPT. BAIRD KILLED

*Last Saturday, Capt. Baird of Merrill's Horse with a
detachment of troops and some enrolled militia,
encountered a band of bushwhackers near Roanoke, in
Howard County. In the skirmish, which was very
slight, the Captain was killed. Beyond this, the Federal
side sustained no damage. Six or eight rebels were
killed, one wounded, and a number taken prisoner. We*

understand Capt. Baird was from Chillicothe, Mo., where he recruited his company.

In addition to the newspaper report, there are also official reports of the skirmish.

HUDSON, MO., September 8, 1862.

Captain [J. W.] Baird, with a few of Merrill's Horse and some Enrolled Militia, attacked guerrilla camp south of Roanoke yesterday [6th?], dispersing them, killing 4, wounding several, capturing 3 prisoners, some horses, arms, &c. Our loss, I regret to say, is Captain Baird, Merrill's Horse, mortally wounded, since dead. No other casualties.

LEWIS MERRILL,

Brigadier-General.

September 26, 1862: Execution in Huntsville

Charles King, Charles Tillotson, and D. S. Washburn were executed at Huntsville, just east of the grounds of Mount Pleasant College (which was at the end of East Library Street in Huntsville). The three men had been accused of guerilla activity after having taken a loyalty oath not to take up arms against the United States. It is possible D.S. Washburn, who was styled a captain at the time of execution was Delaney S. Washburn, who served with the 2nd Northeast Regiment, Missouri Cavalry (Franklin) with the rank of private. No records of Charles Tillotson having been in regular service have been found. Charles King's name is so common as not to be able to identify which regular CSA unit he may have belonged to if any. On September 25th, William Augustus Hall, George Hobbs Burckhartt, and Henry Austin sent a letter to the Union command asking for a reprieve for the three men. This letter went ignored. Some believe the men were buried on the lawn of the Old Randolph County Courthouse. It is more probably they were buried east of the old college where executed, although no evidence supports this. The logical location for burial of course is in the city cemetery. The official reports are below:

HEADQUARTERS NORTHEAST MISSOURI DIVISION, Macon City, Mo., September 23, 1862.

Major A. T. DENNY,

Huntsville, Mo.:

MAJOR: Captain Burkhardt has been directed to take back to Huntsville the following prisoners: Charles King, Charles Tillotson, and D. S. Washburn.

With regard to these men you will observe the order herewith inclosed, which will have such a satisfactory effect that no further execution in your vicinity may be necessary.

I wish the execution of these men to be done with due form and ceremony, and thinking you may not be aware of the proper form, give the following description of how it is to be done:

At the hour fixed for the execution your whole command will be paraded and marched to the execution ground, together with the condemned and the firing party; the firing party will be selected by lot from your men, six men for each prisoner. The march to the execution ground is in the following order; First. A company of your command. Second. The prisoners, each with the firing party in the rear of him. Third. The rest of your command.

Having reached the ground, the command will be formed on three sides of a square, facing inwards. On the open side the prisoners and firing party will be disposed as in the diagram.

24

Before going to the ground the muskets of the firing party will be loaded-not in the presence of the men who are to use them-and of each six one of them will be loaded with a blank cartridge, the others with ball. This is done in order that no individual of the firing party may know to a certainty that his piece contained a ball. The prisoners are then blindfolded and made to kneel before the firing parties, and the commanding officer gives the order, "Ready! aim! fire!:

Six men must be detailed as reserve, whose duty it will be to finish the execution of any one of the prisoners who may not be killed by the first discharge.

Instruct your firing party that they are simply discharging their duty, and however disagreeable it may be it is a duty, and they will show mercy to the prisoners by aiming true at the heart, that the first fire may kill them.

I hope, major, that this solemn execution of a sentence and vindication of violated law may be properly conducted, and that both yourself and your men will do their duty faithfully, however unpleasant it may be.

After the execution the whole command is marched by the dead bodies, and they are then taken up and decently interred.

I am, major, very respectfully, your obedient servant,

LEWIS MERRILL,
Brigadier-General, Commanding.

[Inclosure.]

SPECIAL ORDERS,

HDQRS. NORTHEAST MISSOURI DIVISION,
Numbers 35.

Macon City, Mo., September 23, 1862.

* * * *

II. Charles King, Charles Tillotson, and D. S. Washburn, having once been in arms in rebellion against their lawful Government, and having been pardoned for that offense and taken a solemn oath not again to take up arms against the United States, were afterward found in arms as members of a guerrilla band and taken prisoners, and, in accordance with the laws of war, will be shot at or near Huntsville, Mo., on

26

Friday, the 26th instant, between the hours of 10 a. m. and 3 p. m., having incurred the just penalty of a violated parole and willful and intentional perjury. This sentence will be duly carried into execution by the commanding officer of the troops at Huntsville, for which this shall be his warrant.

III. The following-named prisoners, now in confinement at Macon City, having once been pardoned for the crime of taking up arms against their Government, and having taken a solemn oath not again to take up arms the United States, have been taken in arms, in violation of said oath and their solemn parole, and are therefore ordered to be shot to death on Friday, the 26th of September, between the hours of 10 o'clock a. m. and 3 o'clock p. m.

The commander of the post at Macon City is charged with the execution of the order, and for their execution this shall be his warrant.

Names of prisoners to be executed: Frank E. Drake, Dr. A. C. Rowe, Elbert Hamilton, William H. Earhart, William Searcy, J. A. Wysong, G. H. Fox, Edward Riggs, David Bell, John H. Oldham, James H. Hall.

By order of Brigadier-General Merrill:

27

GEO. M. HOUSTON,
Major and Assistant Adjutant-General.

Chapter Three: 1863

Following the execution of Washburn, Tillotson, and King Randolph County was quiet until September, 1863. In the time between, several arrests a month were made on the charge of aiding the enemy. Among those arrested were Neal Holman, Andrew Baker, Thomas Baker, Madison Baker, Solomon Lewis, Hezekiah Hamilton, D.J. Stamper, Daniel McKinney, T.C. Jackson, and James Matlock. It was also during this time that loyalty oaths were extracted from known Southern Sympathizers, and many men were conscripted into both the Union and Confederate armies. The year overall was very quiet. Looking at newspapers and other records one would hardly know there was a war going on about Randolph County.

September 10, 1863: Thomas Hunter Raids Renick

Thomas Hunter and eight to ten men fired shots at a train on the North Missouri Railroad about three miles north of Sturgeon near the Randolph County line. That same day, they robbed two stores in Renick.(*Guerrilla Warfare in Civil War Missouri, Volume II, 1863*, Nichols)

September 20, 1863: Skirmish Somewhere in the County

The location of the skirmish is unknown other than it took place in a thicket in Randolph County. Confederate Captain Ingham with ten men ambushed Captain William A, Skinner and a patrol of fourteen riders of the First Provisional Enrolled Missouri Militia. The Confederates shot until the militia returned fire, One Union soldier was killed and Captain Skinner was grazed by a bullet. The militia pursued and found the rebel camp. (*Guerrilla Warfare in Civil War Missouri, Volume II, 1863*, Nichols)

Chapter Four: 1864

The relative quiet of 1863 was to be broken in the spring of 1864. That is when Randolph County became a hotbed of guerilla activity. Captain William T. Anderson aka "Bloody Bill" returned to his home county of Randolph, and in the process of doing so raised Hell. He and other guerillas kept the Union regulars on their toes. This was not random activity though. The plan of the guerillas was to keep the Union forces tied down and busy to help General Sterling Price's last bid to take Missouri.

April 1, 1864: Bill Stephen's Raid on Cairo

Not much is known about this raid. Bill Stephens with two other men robbed stores and caused general mischief in Cairo (*Guerrilla Warfare in Civil War Missouri, Volume IV, September 1864–June 1865*, Nichols).

July 15, 1864: Anderson Returns Home

After camping near New Hope Methodist Church at Fort Henry, Captain William T. Anderson and his band road into Huntsville in the early hours. A store safe that held the county treasury and money of many Huntsville residents was robbed of $44,000, and travelling liquor salesmen George Damon was shot behind what is now the Historical Museum. Damon died a short time later in a bed in the Hotel Randolph which stood where the Nan's Tea Room building and the buildings behind it are now. Anderson then returned money to friends he grew up with in town and then left headed south along the Fayette Road.

Official report is as follows:

MACON, July 16, 1864.

Major O. D. GREENE,
Assistant Adjutant-General:

MAJOR: It was a portion of Quantrill's band at Huntsville yesterday; they numbered twenty-two, and stole $45,000 in cash, a portion of which was coin. They killed 1 man, Mr. Damon, of Saint Louis, robbed stores, and plundered indiscriminately from Unionists and rebels. Captain Smith, Ninth Cavalry Missouri State Militia, pursued the parties and came up with them on the Fayette road, ten miles from Huntsville; a running fight of four miles ensued, in which one of the rascals was shot. They were mounted on the best of *horses and soon distanced our jaded party. The road on which the chase occurred was strewn with ribbons, silks, and other items of their plunder. The leader of the villains was once a resident of Huntsville. Dispatched from different sections of the district indicate increasing troubles. The telegraph lines to Saint Joseph are interrupted. I shall try and get through some way.*

CLINTON B. FISK,
Brigadier-General.

July 16, 1864: Skirmish Between Anderson and Union Units

Captain W.T. Anderson and his men left Huntsville on July 15, 1864, and proceeded south on what was then known as the Fayette Road. They stopped at the home of Joel Smith, not far from present day Higbee, pistol whipped him, and stole two horses. After leaving Smith's they continued south on the Fayette Road where they were overtaken by members of the 9th Calvary Missouri State Militia. A running battle ensued with the guerillas out distancing the Union force. The official report is as follows:

MACON, Mo., July 15, 1864.

Col. O.D. Greene, Assistant Adjutant-General:

I have just received the following dispatch from Huntsville, Mo.:

Huntsville was robbed this morning of between seventy-five and one hundred thousand dollars. One man -- citizen -- killed. About thirty-five guerrillas, commanded by BILL ANDERSON, did the work. They left in the direction of Renick. W.R. SAMUEL.

To James D. Head:

I have notified the commanding officer at Sturgeon of the raid. No troops in Randolph County.

JOHN F. WILLIAMS,
Colonel Ninth Cavalry, M.S.M.

"Maj. O. D. GREENE,
Assistant Adjutant-General:

MAJOR: It was a portion of Quantrill's band at Huntsville yesterday; they numbered twenty-two, and stole $45,000 in cash, a portion of which was coin. They killed 1 man, Mr. Damon, of Saint Louis, robbed stores, and plundered indiscriminately from Unionists

34

and rebels. Captain Smith, Ninth Cavalry Missouri State Militia, pursued the parties and came up with them on the Fayette road, ten miles from Huntsville; a running fight of four miles ensued, in which one of the rascals was shot. They were mounted on the best of horses and soon distanced our jaded party. The road on which the chase occurred was strewn with ribbons, silks, and other items of their plunder. The leader of the villains was once a resident of Huntsville. Dispatches from different sections of the district indicate increasing troubles. The telegraph lines to Saint Joseph are interrupted. I shall try and get through some way.

CLINTON B. FISK,"

July 23, 1864: Raid on Renick by Anderson

Having been outside the county, W.T. Anderson and his men returned and raided Renick. They pulled down the telegraph wires, robbed stores, and set fire to the railroad depot. No one was hurt. They rode onto Allen.

July 23, 1864: Skirmish at Allen

After raiding Renick, W. T. Anderson and his men
went to Allen where they attacked the Seventeenth
Illinois Cavalry under the command of Lt, Ebenezer
Knapp. The Seventeenth barricaded themselves in the
railroad depot, and the guerrillas took cover. Some of
Anderson's men made it known that they planned to
attack the train, so some women walked down the
track and warned the coming train. The train backed
down the tracks to Sturgeon. Unable to take the depot,
the band robbed stores and took horses. When all was
said and done two guerrillas were dead .Nine
government horses were killed and seven horses of
civilians. The official reports as follows:

SAINT LOUIS, MO., July 24, 1864.

COMMANDING OFFICER MACON CITY, MO.:

*Report from Allen last night that Lieutenant Knapp
with forty men, re- enforced, fought for an hour with a
party of bushwhackers and lost 20 horses.
Commanding general regrets to hear that more
execution was not done by Lieutenant Knapp and his
men. He trusts that hereafter they will do that work
more effectually. Forty men ought to have killed all the
bushwhackers in a fight of an hour, if a sufficient*

degree of coolness and certainty in firing had been used.

R. S. THOMS,
Captain and Aide- de- Camp.

Report of Lieutenant Ebenezer Knapp, Seventeenth Illinois Cavalry.

HEADQUARTERS,

Glasgow, Mo., September 1, 1864.

GENERAL: I have the honor to report that on Saturday, July 23, 1864, while at Allen, Randolph County, Mo., in command of a detachment of forty men from this post, I was attacked by guerrillas, commanded by Bill Anderson, with nearly double my force. The attack was repelled without the loss of any men, but with the loss of 9 Government horses (killed) and 7 horses belonging to citizens, which had been pressed for the expedition. On the following day, at Huntsville, Randolph County, Mo., a second attack was made on my command, in which 3 Government horses were killed or lost and 12 horses of private citizens lost or killed. We also lost 2 men killed-John

Nicholls, private, Company A, Forty-sixth Regiment Missouri State Militia, and John Daniels, private (blacksmith), of Company H, Seventeenth Illinois Cavalry.

I have the honor to be, your obedient servant,

E. KNAPP,

Second Lieutenant Company G, Seventeenth Illinois Cavalry.

July 24, 1864: Skirmish Between Anderson and Union Units

The exact location of this engagement is unknown other than being three to four miles from Huntsville on the Fayette Road. If W. T. Dameron's account given later is of the same skirmish, the location can be reliably determined. The Seventeenth Illinois Cavalry under Lt. Ebeneezer Knapp was attacked by W.T. "Bloody Bill" Anderson.

Knapp and his men had gone looking for Anderson after the attack on Allen. They stopped in Huntsville and recruited more men, and proceeded down the Fayette Road. When Knapp's men reported Anderson's men along the road, Knapp ordered his men to dismount and form in a line to take the charge. Anderson charged and as the militia's horses were not accustomed to being around gunfire they panicked. In the confusion, the militia managed to return fire and killed one of Anderson's men, and wounded Anderson. Knapp's men then retreated. Two men, John Nicholls, private, Company A, Forty-sixth Regiment Missouri State Militia, and John Daniels, private (blacksmith), of Company H, Seventeenth Illinois Cavalry were killed. Their bodies were mutilated, and a note left on them that read, "You come to hunt bushwhackers, now you are skelpt, Clemyent skelpt you. Wm Anderson." Also lost were 3 government horses and 12 horses of civilians.

It is possible a tale told by W. T. Dameron in a story in the Oct. 5, 1929 edition of the *Moberly Monitor-Index* is about this skirmish. The only thing different in the account of the battle is the name of the commanding officer, The account in condensed form goes as thus:

Levi Hagar was made to give an oath to report to the militia any time he saw Confederate units as it was said he was harboring and aiding guerrillas. He had been good friends with William T. Anderson's family when they had lived southeast of Huntsville in the Hagar school district, and "Bloody Bill" Anderson was known to frequent his home. When Anderson stopped by Hagar's house Hagar told Anderson he would have to report him. Anderson told him that was alright just let them eat. On the way into town near the home of Thomas B. Reed, Hagar met the militia and told them Anderson was in the area. The militia marched south on the Huntsville and Fayette Road in search of Anderson and his men. They reached the Sweet Springs Creek Bridge and a Mr. Shaefer informed them Anderson had passed there. The company went a couple miles more and then turned back thinking Anderson and his men were leaving the county. Near Shaefer's house, the advance guard of the company came upon Anderson who had doubled back behind them. The advance guard fired two shots and then retreated to the rest of the company. When the rest of the company came in sight of Anderson Captain Fin Denny ordered the militia to dismount and form a battle line. Anderson had lined his men up across the road. And then Anderson gave the command to charge. Anderson's men charged yelling and screaming. At this point Denny ordered his men to remount. When the firing began the militia became demoralized with many diving into the brush while others simply fired a couple of shots and ran leaving horses behind. Two militia men were killed, and their names forgotten. A young bushwhacker was also killed by the name of Crewes.

Dameron mentions in his account an engagement had taken place the day before between Federals and Anderson. This could have been the skirmish between Knapp and Anderson at Allen. The two accounts line up rather well with the only significant differences being that the second gives a different commanding officer, and gives details of what lead up to the attack. The different commanding officer can easily be explained. Knapp picked up men from Huntsville, if one of these men was Captain Fin Denny he would be ranking officer. However, he was militia, so when it came time to file the report, Knapp who was a regular would have been the one to file it. Given command's opinion the affair was botched, it might have been better for Knapp to have given Denny credit.

Official Report as follows:

Report of Lieutenant Ebenezer Knapp, Seventeenth Illinois Cavalry.

HEADQUARTERS,

Glasgow, Mo., September 1, 1864.

GENERAL: I have the honor to report that on Saturday, July 23, 1864, while at Allen, Randolph County, Mo., in command of a detachment of forty men from this post, I was attacked by guerrillas, commanded by Bill Anderson, with nearly double my force. The attack was repelled without the loss of any men, but with the loss of 9 Government horses (killed) and 7 horses belonging to citizens, which had been pressed for the expedition. On the following day, at Huntsville, Randolph County, Mo., a second attack was made on my command, in which 3 Government horses were killed or lost and 12 horses of private citizens lost or killed. We also lost 2 men killed-John Nicholls, private, Company A, Forty-sixth Regiment Missouri State Militia, and John Daniels, private (blacksmith), of Company H, Seventeenth Illinois Cavalry.

I have the honor to be, your obedient servant,

E. KNAPP,

Second Lieutenant Company G, Seventeenth Illinois Cavalry.

July 30, 1864: Anderson Tortures Judge David Denny

Confederate Captain W.T. Anderson attempted to lure the militia outside the city of Huntsville. In order to do this he went to the home of Lt. Col. Alexander Denny's elderly father Judge David Denny. There he hung the old man three times from the gate post, and sent a servant into Huntsville to let Denny know he had his father. Lt. Col. Denny had to be held back from rushing out with men to his father's rescue as the townspeople suspected it was a setup for an ambush. Once Anderson realized the militia was not coming he left Denny's father for dead. According to local lore, Judge Denny crawled the two miles into town. Official reports had Anderson holding Huntsville at first:

SAINT JOE, MO., July 30, 1864.

Major-General ROSECRANS:

Lieutenant-Colonel Caldwell, with 150 men, is after Bill Anderson to-day from Macon. I have 500 men scouring through Chariton and Randolph to Allen. Lieutenant-Colonel Caldwell's detachment will join General Douglass as soon as the chase after Anderson is over. I am now concentrating the Ninth Cavalry Missouri State Militia, under Colonel Draper, to take the field without baggage or subsistence and follow Anderson's gang day and night until the villain is exterminated. The people in Randolph, Howard, and Boone have exhibited such apathy in responding to your earnest appeal to help themselves that they really

*deserve scourging to some extent. Colonel Catherwood
has his hands full in Clay.*

*CLINTON B. FISK,
Brigadier-General.*

MEXICO, July 30, 1864.

Major-General ROSECRANS:

*Train from Macon brings news that Bill Anderson has
Huntsville surrounded. Hung Colonel Denny's father
this morning at Huntsville, but let him down before
dead. Troops from Macon City en route for Huntsville.
First Iowa have not reached me yet.*

*J. B. DOUGLASS,
Brigadier-General.*

*AINT LOUIS, Mo., July 30, 1864.
Brigadier-General DOUGLASS,*

Mexico:

*Have telegraphed Fisk about the First Iowa, and asked
troops to watch from Keytesville. You have Bill
Anderson. Use everything you can to destroy him.*

W. S. ROSECRANS,
Major-General.

July 31, 1864: Raid on Church

Jim Anderson raided a church in Northwest Randolph County. The name of the church was not given, nor are any details.

August 7, 1864: Skirmish at Bagby's Farm

Lt. Col. Alexander Denny hearing Jim Anderson was in the area went south with the 46th Enrolled Missouri Militia and a sergeant's detail of the 9th Cavalry Missouri State Militia. They found Anderson and ten men on the farm of Owen Bagby, Denny and his men immediately rushed the farm house, and Anderson and his men fled. In the pursuit, they killed one of Anderson's men and wounded another. Anderson and the rest of the bushwhackers fled into the brush, and scattered.

Here is the official report:

Brigadier-General, Commanding.

Lieutenant Colonel J. F. BELTON,

Assistant Adjutant-General, Camden, Ark.

AUGUST 7, 1864.-Skirmish near Huntsville, Mo.

Report of Lieutenant Colonel Alexander F. Denny, Forty-Sixth Infantry Enrolled Missouri Militia.

HDQRS. FORTY-SIXTH Regiment ENROLLED MISSOURI MIL.,

Huntsville, Mo., August 8, 1864.

GENERAL: I have the pleasure to report that I moved from this place on the morning of the 7th with a small detachment of the Ninth Cavalry Missouri State Militia, commanded by Sergeant Fisher, and detachments of Captain Mayo's and Lieutenant McKinsey's Volunteer Militia, commanded by Lieutenant Dunn. We came upon the trail of Jim Anderson, the notorious robber and guerrilla, some five miles south of this place, about 10 o'clock, and after pursuing it about two hours lost it. I scoured the brush for miles, and at 2 p. m. came out upon the road from Huntsville to Fayette, at the residence of Owen Bagby. Four of our men rode up to the house, when Anderson and his men commenced firing upon them from the house. I ordered the column to dismount and

charge them on foot. The boys came up in fine style,
with a deafening yell, when Anderson mounted his men
and retreated hastily through the rear of the farm,
having previously left the gates down. I ordered the
men to remount, and with some five or six of the men
who had their horses in advance, charged the enemy
as he retreated through the fields. We were obstructed
by gates and fences, and the enemy got under cover of
the woods some 300 yards in advance of us. With the
little handful of men in the advance I ordered a charge
through the thick brush, which was made in gallant
style, random shots being fired at us and returned by
our men until we reached a long lane. Here the chase
became fierce and rapid. We ran upon the rear,
coming on two men mounted on one horse. The horse
was shot from under them, and the men scaled the
fence and took to the pastures. George Raynolds, of
Captain Mayo's company, who was with me in the
advance, having fired hi last shot fell back to reload. A
short hand to-hand conflict with pistols ensued
between the robber and myself, when, after the
exchange of some four or five shots, George Peak,
Company D, Ninth Cavalry Missouri State Militia,
came to my relief and ended his existence with a rifle-
shot. He had been previously wounded in the neck and
back. John Kale, of Company D, Ninth Cavalry
Missouri State Militia, pursued the other dismounted
man on foot through the fields until he had exhausted

47

his last shot, having previously wounded him in the neck. So soon as the men came up I ordered them forward, but Anderson being so well mounted could not be overtaken. The men all conducted themselves well. At the time of the attack we were not fully aware of Anderson's strength. There were only ten men at Bagby's, yet their number was reported to us subsequently at thirty men. Result of the skirmish, 1 man killed and 1 mortally wounded; also Jim Anderson reported shot through the nose; 1 horse killed, 1 wounded, and 1 captured; also 1 gun and 4 or 5 pistols. Money taken from the person of the dead man: $90 in gold, $286 in greenbacks, $4.50 in silver, $16 W. M. B.; total, $396.50. Our loss, 1 horse. Anderson turned into the brush after a run of three miles and scattered his men. We followed the trail as long as we could, when we turned in the direction of Huntsville. We came upon his again at 6 o'clock in the brush within three miles of Huntsville. A few shots were fired by our men and an exciting chase of ten minutes followed, when the enemy was lost in the thick brush.

I am, very respectfully, your obedient servant,

A. F. DENNY,
Lieutenant Colonel Forty-sixth Regiment Enrolled Missouri Militia.

September 10, 1864: Skirmish Near Roanoke

Major King and members of the Sixth Cavalry, Missouri State Militia attacked Clifton Holtzclaw's guerrilla band near Roanoke. The official reports are as follows:

SEPTEMBER 10, 1864.- Skirmish near Roanoke, Mo.

REPORTS.

Numbers 1.- Brigadier General Clinton B. Fisk, U. S. Army, commanding District of North Missouri.

Numbers 2.- Major Austin A. King, jr., Sixth Missouri State Militia Cavalry.

Numbers 1. Report of Brigadier General Clinton B. Fisk, U. S. Army, commanding District of North Missouri.

SAINT JOSEPH, September 11, 1864.

The detachment sent out from Glasgow yesterday under Major King, Sixth Cavalry, Missouri State Militia, attacked Holtzclaw's band, numbering sixty, just east of Roanoke,in Howard County, and revolvers were captured. In the chase 2 of our men were wounded, 1 severely. The First Iowa are stirring up the bushwhackers in Boone.

CLINTON B. FISK,
Brigadier- General.

Colonel O. D. GREENE,

Asst. Adjt. General and Chief of Staff, Saint Louis.

Numbers 2. Report of Major Austin A. King, jr., Sixth Missouri State Militia Cavalry.

FAYETTE, September 11, 1864.

I came upon Holtzclaw's command yesterday east of Roanoke, in Howard County. They numbered about sixty men. They did not stand long against my advance under command of Captain Turner, who charged them as soon as he came upon them. A running fight of five miles ensued, in which we killed 6 and wounded several men, captured 6 horses, and at least a dozen shotguns, with a loss of 2 of my men wounded, 1 severely. I will move again to- morrow, my horses being now badly run down.

AUSTIN A. KING, JR.,
Major, &.

General FISK.

ADDENDA.

SAINT JOSEPH, September 11, 1864.

Major KING,

Commanding Sixth Cav. Mo. State Militia, in the Field, Glasgow:

I congratulate you on the good beginning of the bushwhacking campaign. Strike with vigor and determination. Take no prisoners. We have enough of that sort on hand now. Pursue and kill. I have two of Holtzclaw's men, just captured. They state that he camps, when in Howard County, in the rear of old man Hackley's farm, not far from Fayette.make a dash in there at night and get him if possible. Let a detachment secretly watch his mother's residence. He is home almost daily, and his sisters are great comforters of the bushwhackers. Old man Hackley has a son in the brush. I shall soon send out of the district the bushwhacking families. Go ahead and give us a good report.

CLINTON B. FISK,
Brigadier- General.

September 25, 1864: Anderson Tries to Intimidate Huntsville Garrison

Guerrillas under the command of W.T. Anderson and George M. Todd arrived outside Huntsville with 250 men and demanded the militia surrender. Lt. Col Alexander Denny had detachments of Missouri's 9th Missouri State Militia Cavalry and 46th Enrolled Militia in Huntsville, and Major King and the 13th Cavalry Missouri Volunteers were approaching from the south. Denny's response to Anderson's demands was "come in and take it." Anderson and Todd retreated leaving the town unharmed. They then went east and then down the North Missouri Railroad tearing down telegraph lines. The official report as follows:

HUNTSVILLE, September 26, 1864.

General C. B. FISK:

Thrailkill, Todd & Co., were here yesterday at 12 o'clock. A demand for the surrender of the place was

*made in the name of Colonel Perkins. I told them to
come and take it. They reported their number at 500; I
suppose they had 250. They went in the direction of
Renick; were four miles northwest of here when last
heard from.*

*A. F. DENNY,
Lieutenant-Colonel.*

October 13-27, 1864: Union Raid on Milton

Union 1st Lt. Charles W. Watts lead his men on a
murdering spree through Randolph County killing 15
men accused of harboring guerrillas around Milton.
The soldiers also raided Milton robbing W. E.
Briscoe's store. (October 22, 1864 edition of *Saint
Louis Daily Democrat*)

Endword: The End of the War

As can be seen, the guerilla war in Randolph County which was hot and heavy in 1864 ended as abruptly as it began. With the death of W.T. Anderson on October 26, 1864 in Richmond, Missouri one of the major agitators in Randolph County was gone. Only days before, on the 23rd, General Sterling Price's army had been shattered at the Battle of Westport. Guerilla band leaders were gradually killed or arrested. The failure of General Sterling Price's last drive into Missouri took away one of the purposes of the guerillas, and that was to keep Union forces occupied so they could not fight against Price's army.

By then end of 1864, there were no more raids or skirmishes of note in Randolph County. And by December 16, 1864, the war hardly appeared on the front page of the local papers. The front page of the *Fulton Telegraph* barely mentioned the war, and in the April 18, 1865 edition of *The Macon Gazette*, the primary headline of the front page was "The Temperance Cause." The war had been relegated to brief snippets, or other parts of the newspaper. That is not to say things had returned to normal. What was "normal" for the citizens of Randolph County would never exist again. The slaves were freed, thus bankrupting some farmers who no longer had the hands to farm their fields. With the end of the war, the village of Smithland actually ceased to exist. It was gone with the fortunes of its founder Joel Smith whose settlement had already been hurt by the railroad passing it by.

Overall however, Randolph County had fared very well during the war. Its reconstruction was rapid with a new railroad being completed in 1867 going east from Brunswick through Huntsville to the fledgling town of Moberly. In the following years, Moberly's growth would be rapid, and in 1872, what would become the Wabash Shops came to the county bringing much needed jobs and money. This was a far cry from the hardships seen by those of the Deep South.

The Civil War left its scars in the county however. Many veterans had been wounded, some crippled for life. Racism was a common thing with lynchings taking place in the years that followed. But gradually the county would heal, and become what it is today.

Appendix I: Units Active in the County

This is not an exhausted list of units active in Randolph County, but merely those named in the official combat reports. Please note, some guerilla units are not listed due to their loose organization, and a general lack of information on them. In general, Confederate regulars were not very active in Randolph County.

Union Units

1st Regiment, Iowa Cavalry

In 1864 the 1st Regiment, Iowa Cavalry was assigned to the Union Headquarters in Macon County. They then conducted operations against guerillas in Randolph and Howard Counties.

They were organized in Davenport, Iowa between July 30 and September 12, 1862. The unit was mustered out in Austin, Texas on March 16, 1866.

2nd Missouri Volunteer Cavalry (Merrill's Horse)

Raised under the authority of Major General John C. Fremont Merrill's Horse was a volunteer unit, but one that its commanding officer Captain Lewis Merrill demanded strict military discipline of. Merrill himself was not a volunteer, but a U.S. Army regular.

Merrill's Horse was organized from September 2 to December 11, 1861. It saw extensive combat in Northeast and Central Missouri as well as in other parts of the state. The entire regiment was never active in Randolph County, however detachments harassed guerillas in the county, and there was a skirmish between a detachment of Merrill's Horse and guerillas at Roanoke.

4th Ohio Cavalry

The 4th Ohio Cavalry was organized at Cincinnati, Lima, and Camp Dennison near Cincinnati from August to November 1861. The unit saw service in Central Missouri for a short amount of time and detachments of it saw action at the Battle of Roan's Tan Yard.

9th Calvary Missouri State Militia

The 9th MSM Cavalry was raised by Colonel Odon Guitar and organized starting February 12, 1862. Beginning in February, 1862 it was assigned to the District of North Missouri where it saw extensive action against guerillas in Randolph and surrounding counties. The Missouri State Militia was unusual in that while being a militia, they were equipped by the Federal government. This meant overall they were better equipped and trained than most militias. The 9th was largely recruited from North Missouri with many men from Randolph, Chariton, and Howard serving in its companies.

17th Illinois Cavalry.

The 17th Illinois Cavalry was organized beginning September 11, 1863 The Second Battalion of the regiment saw some action in Randolph and surrounding counties.

46th Enrolled Missouri Militia

Organized from August 4 to November 29, 1862 the 46th EMM was eventually based in Huntsville under the command of Randolph County native Colonel Alexander F. Denny. Companies C, D, F, G, H, I, as well as a detached company under the command of Captain James McKinsey were largely composed of men from Randolph County. Other companies were made up of men mainly from Howard County. Its initial commanders were Colonels Thomas J. Barthelow and Clark H. Goren. The unit was reorganized between June 10, 1863 and May 12, 1865.

In the final years of the war, the 46th was used to garrison Huntsville, and this prevented raids by guerillas.

66th Illinois Volunteer Infantry Regiment

Originally known as Birge's Sharpshooters, they were later redesignated Western Sharpshooters-14th Missouri Volunteers. They were mustered into service on November 23, 1861.

The 66th during the early months of 1862 was assigned to guard the North Missouri Railroad. This allowed them to see some action in Randolph County.

Confederate Units

5th Regiment, 3rd Division Missouri State Guard

This unit was John A. Poindexter's unit, and saw activity at the Battle of Carthage and Wilson's Creek. It is also the one that held up the train at Allen. It is possible the recruits at Roan's Tan Yard were members of this unit. Unfortunately, not much else is known of it. Records of Confederate units are scarce.

Anderson's Partisan Rangers

The only large unit of guerillas to operate in Randolph County was the one under the command of Captain William T. Anderson aka "Bloody Bill." Captain George M. Todd with his men was also in Randolph County along with Anderson and his men at one point. But the combined forces never made any raids or fought any skirmishes in Randolph County as they had done elsewhere. The history of the unit is well known, its activities being rather infamous. At various times Anderson had as few as 35 men, upwards to well over 75 men.

William Quantrill was given a commission in the Confederate Army under the Partisan Ranger Act in 1861. Anderson joined Quantrill's band in early 1863. In the summer of that year he was made a lieutenant serving under George M. Todd. Shortly after, he was made a captain in command of 30 to 40 men. In late 1863, after a dispute with Quantrill in Texas, Anderson returned to Missouri with his own band of men, and began operations in Central Missouri.

In Randolph County, Anderson led raids on Allen, Huntsville, and Renick. He and his guerillas also fought skirmishes south of Huntsville, at Allen, and west of what is now Higbee. The band's last known major activity in Randolph County was an attempt to make the local garrison at Huntsville surrender only a few days before the Centralia Massacre. The unit's most infamous deeds after parting with Quantrill were the Centralia Massacre and the Battle of Centralia in which over 100 Union soldiers died on September 27, 1864. Archie Clement took command of the unit after Anderson's death on October 25, 1864. The group splintered by mid-November of that same year.

Appendix II: Biographies

The number of men that served in the Union and Confederate Armies, not to mention those that fought as bushwhackers are too numerous for each to be given a biography in a volume as small as this. Therefore, only those that were in command of units that operated within the county are covered here. Even then many are still left out. There were many captains of companies in the county for which there is little to no information. Therefore, only those that saw major combat or were in overall command are listed here. Biographies of everyone else will have to wait for another book.

Captain William T. Anderson aka "Bloody Bill" (Cofederate)

It is not clear where William T. Anderson better know as "Bloody Bill" Anderson was born. What is clear is he was a child of William and Martha Anderson, and that they came to Randolph County sometime in 1840. As William T. was born that year it is possible he was born in or around Huntsville, Missouri, or he may have been born in Hopkins County, Kentucky; Jefferson County, Missouri; Palmyra, Missouri; or in transit. He spent his entire childhood in and around Huntsville, not leaving the area until he was around 17 when the family moved to Kansas. He had two brothers, Ellis and James both who were younger as well as younger sisters Mary C. Josephine, and Martha.

The Anderson family lived in various places in and around Huntsville during the almost twenty years they were here. The first place they lived was known as the old Hunt farm, adjoining the old Joseph M. Hammett farm a mile or two north of Huntsville off of what is now Route C. They then lived in Huntsville around the area of what is now the junction of West Depot and

Hance Street. They last lived in the county south of town in the area of the old Hagar School. Anderson attended school there and a school in Huntsville which was near the corner of Oak and Mulberry Streets.

William T.'s father was a hatter by profession, and went to seek gold in 1850 in California, but returned empty handed as so many of the men from Randolph County who went as a group did. William T. was described as a quiet boy who liked to hunt and play with bows and arrows. He seemed to have been of no problem to anyone in the town of Huntsville. In essence his childhood was unremarkable and uneventful, most often described as well behaved, not unlike many other children of the time period. The family was well respected in Huntsville, the father being a member of the I.O.O.F. Lodge. In 1857 the Andersons moved to the area of Agnes City, Kansas.

The family was well respected in Agnes City (near Council Grove) and by 1860 William T. co-owned a 320 acre farm. Once settled there the Andersons became friends with Judge Arthur Ingham Baker another Southerner. On June 28, 1860, William T.'s mother Martha was killed after being struck by lightning. Sometime around this time things began to unravel for the Andersons. Ellis shot and killed a Native American and had to flee to Iowa.

William T. is said to have killed a member of the Kaw tribe in self-defense because the Native American tried to rob him. Nevertheless, William T. joined a freight hauling business with his father, and started dealing in horses. At some point Anderson either began dealing in stolen horses or stealing horses himself and selling them along the Santa Fe Trail. The demand for horses had become rather high with the outbreak of the Civil War, and they were a valuable commodity. In late 1861, William T. and Judge A.I. Baker attempted to join the Confederate Army, but were attacked by the 6th Kansas Cavalry. Anderson escaped, but Baker was captured and spent several months in prison. Either before or after Baker's time in prison he had begun courting Mary Ellen Anderson, but broke it off to marry Annis Segur. It was not long after this that William T.'s father was killed.

Accounts vary as to how it happened. Some accounts have it that his father and uncle were hung by Jayhawkers on March 11, 1862 while William T. and his brother Jim were out delivering cattle to Fort Leavenworth. The brothers returned to find their father and uncle hanging, the house burned, and their possessions gone. Another account has that A.I. Baker shot and killed the elder Anderson. This account goes that after Baker had been captured by the 6th Kansas

Cavalry he became a Union man. In May of 1862 he issued an arrest warrant for someone named Lee Griffin. William C., William T.'s father went to Agnes City to confront Judge Baker over the warrant as well as Baker's having wronged Mary Ellen Anderson and in the confrontation was shot by Baker. William T. was arrested for hiding Griffin and horse thieving, but was then released, and given a lawyer. Anderson left for home and remained there until he learned Judge Baker would not be charged for killing his father. He, his brother Jim, and Lee Griffin then went to Agnes City on July 21, 1862 and burned Baker and Baker's brother in law George Segur alive in a store they had fled into to hide after a brief gun battle. They then burned Baker's home, stole two horses, and headed for Missouri.

Accounts of William T. Anderson aka "Bloody Bill" during the Civil War vary depending on the writer. Some portray him as a cutthroat and murderer that raped young black women, took scalps, and killed people just to see them die. Other accounts simply portray him as a man bent on revenge for the death of his father and the death of his sister Josephine and driven by disgust at the atrocities committed on Missouri Southerners.

One must keep in mind that there were many atrocities committed by both sides during the Civil War. There were Union forces that committed almost as serious a crimes as "Bloody Bill" that are no longer written about. The Sacking of Osceola is one such case. On September 23, 1861 the town of Osceola, Missouri was plundered and burned to the ground by James H. Lane and his band of Jayhawkers. At least nine civilians were killed. It is said this raid was what lead to the Lawrence, Kansas Massacre being done in retaliation. The town of Pleasant Hill. Missouri was burned by Charles Jennison and his band of Jayhawkers on November 17, 1861. Jayhawkers also burned the towns of Dayton, and Nevada, Missouri. At Kingsville, Missouri the town was burned and nine men killed. In September of 1864 Martin Rice, his son, along with six neighbors were captured by the 9th Kansas Cavalry. The six neighbors, all civilians were murdered, but Rice and his son were spared.

In light of this, "Bloody Bill" Anderson was no different than many other men of the period, though he admittedly was perhaps more blood thirsty. No doubt though both Jayhawker and Bushwhacker justified what they were doing as retaliation for the last "Lawrence" or the last "Osceola." Anderson was a man in a war where atrocities were being committed on both sides. He saw death all around him, and he was one among many that were dealing out death.

That being said, William T. Anderson was no hero. He executed an entire company of men who were unarmed. He kept scalps of men he killed tied to his saddle. It is said he allowed his men to rape female slaves. And even Southern slaveholders were not spared being beaten and having their horses taken.

After killing Baker, William T. and his brother Jim joined with a man named Bill Reed and began raiding. At this point it is not clear whether they preyed on just Unionists or Confederate sympathizers as well. Later accounts have William Quantrill rebuking them for stealing from Confederate sympathizers. The story goes that Quantrill sent out a detachment that captured Bill and Jim, took their horses, and told them not to prey on Southerners.

The Andersons and Reed then began operating between Lexington and Warrensburg, Missouri. In May, 1863 Anderson joined Quantrill's Raiders near Council Grove, Kansas. In the summer he was promoted to a lieutenant in Quantrill's band. He took part in raids on Westport and Kansas City, Missouri.

By late July Anderson was a captain leading his own men, although still under Quantrill's command. His second in command was Archie Clement a man known to enjoy torture and mutilation. In August of 1863 General Thomas Ewing Jr. had the female relatives of bushwhackers arrested. On August 13, 1863 the building they were being kept in collapsed killing Anderson's sister Joshephine who was only 14. Also seriously injured were his sisters Mary Ellen who was 16 and Janie who was only 10. Anderson it was said was convinced it was no accident.

It was not long after on August 21, 1863 that Quantrill attacked Lawerence, Kansas. The objective was to capture or kill Jayhawker leader James H. Lane. Lane it is said hid in a cornfield in his nightshirt. Anderson supposedly said, "I am here for revenge." Regardless, it was the largest number of Bushwhackers assembled during the war. Between 185 and 200 men and boys were killed among them 18 unmustered Union army recruits. Some authors maintain Anderson's unit was responsible for most of the carnage. It could be that Quantrill had planned a less bloody thirsty raid. Some accounts state Anderson gave the order to kill every man and boy big enough to carry a gun. This can perhaps be marked as the first clear sign of Anderson's desire to kill. It was shortly after his sister Josephine was killed, and there had been no killing on this scale prior.

Following the raid, Quantrill and his men Anderson among them went to the area of Mineral Springs, Texas to stay for the winter. While in Texas, Anderson married a woman named Bush Smith of Sherman, Texas. Anderson stayed in Sherman in a house there, and had one child who died as an infant. Tensions between Anderson and Quantrill began to develop with Anderson eventually having Quantrill arrested for the murder of a Confederate officer. Quantrill escaped and Anderson was ordered to capture him, but gave up pursuit. He returned to the camp of the Confederate regulars and received a commission of captain from General Sterling Price. Anderson broke with Quantrill at this point and began to operate on his own command. After several months in Texas Anderson and his men returned to Missouri and began raiding Cooper and Johnson Counties primarily robbing local residents. In July of 1864 Anderson moved his operations to Carroll and Randolph Counties.

On July 15, 1864 "Bloody Bill" Anderson returned home. After camping near New Hope Church in Fort Henry about five miles west of Huntsville, Missouri he entered the town. There he shot one man he suspected of being a U.S. Marshall or in the least a Union spy and his men robbed the depository of $40,000 though some of the money was returned. The man shot, an E.A. Damon of St. Louis was a travelling salesman that tried to run. Otherwise, the raid seemed uneventful. It is unclear whether this was the time that Anderson saved the life of an old schoolmate. A tale told by Margaret Block of the Huntsville Historical Society about her uncle Hayden Rutherford goes that Rutherford was about to be hung by some of Anderson's men for trying to retrieve a horse they had stolen. Anderson rode up and said, "Don't hang him boys. He always helped me with my schoolwork." Anderson then told Rutherford, "I'll see you get your horse back." A few months later Rutherford woke to find the horse in his yard.

Upon leaving Huntsville, Anderson and his band traveled south to Smithland where they stole two horses from Joel Smith and pistol whipped him. The Ninth Cavalry Missouri State Militia under Clinton B. Fisk which was in pursuit overtook Anderson and his men, ten miles from Huntsville on the Fayette Road according to the official report. It is taken though that the Old State Road that also lead to Fayette that was meant as it went through Smith's property while the Fayette Road was to the west. At that point a running fight of four miles took place ending when the band outdistanced the militia.

Eight days later Anderson and his men arrived at Renick, Missouri. With about 65 men he robbed stores, tore down telegraph lines, and burned the railroad depot. They then moved north to the next depot at Allen, Missouri (in what is now Moberly). There they engaged the 17th Illinois Cavalry who took shelter in a fort. All the bushwhackers were able to do was kill the Union force's horses before reinforcements arrived. After this Anderson's band of raids did small raids. In August 13, 1864 they engaged Union militia forcing them to flee in Ray County. On August 30th they were engaged with another Union militia and then pursued by the 4th Missouri Volunteer Cavalry. In September Anderson met up with Quantrill along with George Todd, another guerrilla leader. Anderson convinced them to attack the Union garrison stationed at Fayette, Missouri. On Sept. 24th, the raiders approached the town clad in Union uniforms. The members of the 9th Cavalry, Missouri State Milita that were there were mostly wounded and sick, and only 20 to 25 could fight. They barricaded themselves in barracks made of railroad ties and heavily fortified. Only 75 of the 250 raiders present took part in the attack and they made three charges on the barracks being repelled each time. They broke off the attack after losing five men and only killing two Union soldiers. Anderson and Todd headed north on the Glasgow Road (current Highway

5), while Quantrill went to a camp near Boonesboro in Howard County.

On September 26th Anderson and Todd and their men camped near Centralia, Missouri. On September 27th with 75 men Anderson went into Centralia. While there they looted the town. They found a large amount of whiskey and began drinking. They stopped a stagecoach and robbed its passengers among them being Congressmen James S. Rollins, but Rollins managed to conceal his identity. While they robbed the stage or shortly thereafter a train arrived and the raiders forced it to stop. On board were 23 Union soldiers. Anderson told his men to leave the women alone as they stole about $9,000 from the men on the train. They then forced the 23 Union soldiers to disrobe and took their uniforms. Anderson had the soldiers line up. Anderson selected a sergeant for a potential prisoner swap. When asked what to do with the remaining soldiers Anderson gave his men the order to "parole them." After shooting all the soldiers, Anderson told the civilians they could leave, but not to move the bodies.

It is said Anderson said that the Centralia Massacre was in retaliation for Confederate regulars executed at Palmyra, Missouri. It is also said he had vowed to kill two Union soldiers for every Confederate soldier killed. They then derailed a work train and returned to camp. Upon returning to camp they learned of an approaching Union force coming from Paris, Missouri. The 39th Missouri Volunteer Infantry under the command of Major A.V.E. Johnston with 155 Union soldiers had arrived in Centralia, and Johnston enraged by the massacre went in pursuit of Anderson leaving 35 of his men in the town. Anderson set up an ambush for the Union forces by sending decoys to lure the 39th into a trap. Johnston pursued the decoys and when he saw about 80 men at the base of the hill. Johnston ordered his men to dismount and had every fifth man to hold the horses. Seeing the Union forces dismount the Bushwhackers attacked. Five raiders were killed in the initial charge. After the first attack Anderson had 100 men attack from the flanks. The battle was over rather quickly and almost none of Johnston's troops survived. Besides being dismounted, and out manned, the Union forces had only single shot Enfield muzzle loaders while Anderson's men were armed with revolvers. Following the battle Anderson and his men took scalps and mutilated the bodies. Between the Battle of Centralia and the Centralia Masscare the same day 120 to 140 Union soldiers died with only a handful of survivors.

Following the Battle of Centralia Anderson spent his time evading Union forces intent on capturing or killing him. He kept his troops to the brush often going through ravines, and other places Union forces would not pursue for fear of ambush. In retaliation for the Centralia Massacre Union forces burned the town of Rocheport long considered a safe haven for Bushwhackers. In October of 1864, Anderson and his men met with General Sterling Price at Boonville. Price ordered Anderson and his men to take the scalps and other war trophies off their horses and from their belts. While Anderson was there Price ordered Anderson to raid the North Missouri Railroad and destroy the North Missouri Railroad Bridge. The Bushhwackers then went to Glasgow, Missouri arriving there on October 21, 1864. On October 15th Confederate regulars had shelled the town forcing the Union garrison to surrender. The two Confederate brigades had then left to rejoin Price's army leaving Glasgow unprotected by either Union or Confederate regulars. Qauntrill and his raiders then came to town and stole a large amount of money. Then Anderson arrived and showed up at the mansion of Benjamin Lewis a wealthy Unionist along with his orderly Ike Berry. Anderson severely beat him demanding money and raped a young female slave before enough money was raised to buy Anderson off. Then in the morning Anderson and his men returned whereupon his men raped two more female slaves. Within a few weeks a reporter for the Missouri Democrat out of Saint Louis interviewed Mr. Lewis and his wife about the attack and the account was soon published in the New York Times. Anderson and his men then went northwest leaving Central Missouri behind.

After the Centralia Massacre the Union Army had assigned Lt. Colonel Samuel P. Cox and a group of experienced soldiers to eliminate Anderson and his men. Once Anderson left Glasgow Cox pursued him. On October 26th, Anderson and his men arrived near Richmond, Missouri. The next day they went to Albany, Missouri and pursued a Union force. They rode into a volley of rifle and pistol fire at which point they halted short except for Anderson and another. Anderson was shot down, but the other bushwhacker managed to flee on foot. The other raiders quickly retreated. Anderson and his men had been caught in the same sort of trap he would have arranged. Lt. Colonel Cox had sent the force Anderson was pursing out as a decoy in order to lure Anderson and his men into an ambush, The Union soldiers took the body to the courthouse where it was photographed, beheaded it, and displayed the head on a telegraph pole. They then buried Anderson near Richmond in a field. In 1908 Cole Younger reburied Anderson's body, and in 1967 a memorial stone was set up. Archie Clement took command of Anderson's unit but they soon disintegrated with some joining Quantrill. His brother

Jim survived along with his remaining sisters. They moved to Texas where Jim married William T.'s widow.

The William T. Anderson Huntsville knew was quite different than the William T. Anderson Kansas seemed to know before the war. In Missouri he was a member of a well-respected family. In Kansas he was accused of horse stealing and suspected of murder. Certainly after his father was killed, and certainly after his sister Josephine was killed he changed. But this does not explain why he was accused of dealing in stolen horses in Kansas prior to the war. Perhaps his mother's death changed him, or she was his moral compass. It is as if one were looking at two different people. The boy Huntsville knew was a well behaved young man with whom no one had problems and seemed well enough liked, and the man in Kansas that seemed troublesome with a bad name. It is difficult to reconcile the two. Almost as difficult as reconciling the William T. Anderson some authors portray as a hero, and the "Bloody Bill" Anderson others portray as a cruel blood thirsty killer. We will perhaps never know the truth. One thing is certain, he killed many during a time of chaos and atrocities. In that he may have been no better or worse than many others.

Lt. Col. Alexander Denny (Union)

Information about Alexander Finley Denny is sparse despite for a period of three years he was perhaps the most important man in Huntsville. He was born in the section of Howard County, Missouri that would become Randolph County in 1827 the son of David Rice Denny and Rebecca (Rowland) Denny. His father, a veteran of the War of 1812, was an early settler and arrived in Howard County with his father Alexander Denny, a veteran of the Revolutionary War, in 1818. David Rice Denny later served as a judge in Randolph County. Alexander attended Missouri University in Columbia, Missouri and graduated from the Law School of Harvard University in 1850. He then practiced law in Huntsville in partnership with Thomas B. Reed (who would later become a Missouri State Senator) until joining the militia in 1862. He married Martha McDowell Pitts December 5, 1855. She died March 15, 1857, and was buried in the Pitts Family Cemetery in Randolph County near Yates. He then married Sophia Elizabeth Pitts July 20, 1858. By Sophia he had Eleanor M. Denny, Younger Rice Denny, Rebecca Anna Denny (she died when she was three), George W. Denny (he died when he was four), Mary (Denny) Gordon, and Sophia Emily Denny who did not live long.

On August 21, 1862, after Missouri had been involved in the Civil War for nearly a year the Enrolled Missouri Militia was formed. Denny raised a company of men for the Union that became a part of the 46th Regiment, Enrolled Missouri Militia. He was originally Captain of Company C of this regiment, but by October 1, 1862 he held the rank of Major and was military commander of Huntsville. Charles F. Mayo was promoted from Second Lieutenant to Captain to take charge of Company C. On Dec. 22, 1862 Denny was promoted to Lieutenant Colonel. Sometime after February 3, 1863 he became a part of the 1st Provisional Regiment, Enrolled Missouri Militia. Unlike the Enrolled Missouri Militia, the Provisional Enrolled Militia was a full time force on active duty. Enrolled Missouri Militia often spent time garrisoning towns, were only called on when a need arose, and did not often see combat while the Provisional Enrolled Militia was considered a combat unit. During his time with the 1st Provisional Lt. Colonel Denny saw action against General Shelby of the Confederate Army from September 22 to October 26, 1863. At other times he was in the field combating guerrillas. He left active duty with this unit November 17, 1863.

After the operations against General Shelby some of Lt. Colonel Denny's time was spent in administrative duties trying to maintain law and order, or simply managing the logistics of the war in the area. Such was the case when in November of 1863 when he asked his commanding officers what to do with commissary stores (including 11 tons of beans) left in Mexico, Missouri with no soldiers there to eat them. Another time in November of 1863 while still a major he had to inquire into the release of two prisoners of war who had served under Colonel Poindexter of the Confederate Army. It had been promised they would be released, but had not appeared at their homes yet.

After leaving the 1st Provisional Regiment, Denny returned to the 46th Regiment, Enrolled Missouri Militia on April 21, 1864, and once again was in command of Huntsville. During this time he had at least three interactions with the Andersons. The first was a skirmish with Jim Anderson and about ten bushwhackers On August 7, 1864 Lt. Colonel Denny learned Jim Anderson was close by. With the 46th Regiment, Enrolled Missouri Militia and a detachment of the 9th Cavalry Missouri State Militia (unlike the 46th they were seasoned guerrilla fighters) he found him at Owen Bagby's farm about five miles south of Huntsville. Upon approaching Bagby's house the guerrillas began firing. Lt. Colonel Denny and his men then charged Anderson and his ten men at which point the bushwhackers fled. They continued to pursue them for some distance until they lost them in the brush. No Union troops were killed and one bushwhacker was.

On July 31, 1864. William T. Anderson aka "Bloody Bill" sought to take Huntsville, by luring the militia outside the city. In order to do this he went to the home of Lt. Col. Alexander Denny's elderly father Judge David Denny. There he hung the old man three times from the gate post, and sent a servant into Huntsville to let Denny know he had his father. Lt. Col. Denny had to be held back from rushing out with men to his father's rescue as the townspeople suspected it was a setup for an ambush. Once Anderson realized the militia was not coming he left Denny's father for dead. According to local lore, Judge Denny crawled the two miles into town. Another significant interaction took place September 25, 1865 when Bill Anderson again tried to lure the militia out of Huntsville. He sent an ultimatum demanding the militia surrender the town that he had signed, "Col. Perkins." Denny's response was, "come in and take it." He had all four companies of the 46th Enrolled Missouri Militia stationed in the town, and both the college and courthouse were fortified. According to former guerrillas, Anderson wanted to try to take the town anyway stating these were only local militia. His joint commander, George Todd though, perhaps remembering the Battle of Fayette the day before said they should not. Anderson heeded Todd's advice and they road on. The note said there were 500 in their number, but Denny put the estimate at 250. Major Austin with his companies of guerrilla fighters arrived an hour after the bushwhackers left, but their horses were tired so they could not pursue.

Denny could have encountered the Anderson's another time, but was away from Huntsville. Where Lt. Colonel Denny and the 42nd Enrolled Militia were during Bloody Bill Anderson's raid on Huntsville is unknown. One much later newspaper account said they had gone to Allen on a false report Bloody Bill Anderson was there. All that is known is Huntsville was not garrisoned at the time of the raid, and it is possible the militia was ordered elsewhere.

The rest of the war saw Lt. Colonel Denny only seeing actions with small bands of guerrillas, and continuing to do his administrative duties. Lt. Colonel Denny left active duty on March 14, 1865, and returned to his law practice. Sometime between 1875 and 1880 he left Huntsville and moved to Kansas City. His second wife Sophia died December 16, 1875 and is buried in the Huntsville City Cemetery.

He is shown as practicing law in Kansas City in 1880. He died sometime in 1886 and is buried in Elmwood

Cemetery in Kansas City next to his son Younger Rice Denny. For all his activity in Randolph County for most of his life there is relatively little written on Lt. Colonel Denny. Most of what exists are advertisements for his law firm in the local papers, and then his official record in the military.

He was born in what would shortly become Randolph County into a family that had came here early. His father is listed in the histories as one of the earliest settlers in the county. He was an attorney for twelve years before the war in Huntsville in partnership with a man who become a State Senator. And he achieved the rank of Lt. Colonel and oversaw Huntsville's defenses for much of the war. However, this was a time of divided loyalties. Many Southern Sympathizers had Oaths of Allegiance extracted from them, even as their sons served for the South. Still others were conscripted into service against their will, and there are records to show Lt. Colonel Denny's 46th Regiment, Enrolled Missouri Militia was the destination of many of these drafted men in the county. It was also under his command of the defenses at Huntsville, Confederate Captain Samuel Delaney Washburn was executed at Huntsville. It could be resentments carried over from the war saw to it his name was not mentioned in the 1884 histories of the county. Later histories probably neglected to mention him because his story has been lost to time. It is a shame as no doubt he protected Huntsville from more raids by guerrillas intent on pillaging the town and deserved to be remembered.

Brigadier General Joseph Beeler Douglass (Union)

General J.B. Douglass was born in Mercer County, Kentucky on November 12, 1819 to William Douglass and Frances Jamison Douglass. William Douglass came to Boone County in 1829 and settled not far from Harrisburg. J.B. remained with his father until 1848 when he became a deputy sheriff under Sheriff William P. Hickman. He was elected sheriff in 1850 and reelected in in 1852. In 1856 he was elected to the Missouri General Assembly. In 1862, he was commissioned as Colonel of the 61st Enrolled Missouri Militia.

In 1862, he was commissioned a Brigadier General and assigned to the Eight Military District of which Randolph County was a part. Most of his time was spent in administrative duties, and his name is seen often on reports for the region. In 1866, Douglass was made United States assessor of the Fourth District. In 1868, he left that position and went into the nursery business. He died August 20, 1898.

Major General Clinton Bowen Fisk (Union)

Clinton B. Fisk was born December 8, 1828 in
Livingston County, New York. His family then moved
to Coldwater, Michigan. He attended college and then
went into business as a merchant, miller, and banker.
The Panic of 1857 ruined him financially and he
moved to Saint Louis, Missouri.

Fisk was involved in the war from the time it was
started in Missouri being with the home guard that
seized Camp Jackson in May 1861 Fisk was appointed
colonel of the 33rd Missouri Volunteer Infantry of the
Union Army on September 5, 1862. On November 24,
1862, he was promoted to Brigadier General. During
the war Fisk first served with the District of Southeast
Missouri and later the Department of North Missouri.
Being with the Department of North Missouri placed
him in command of Randolph County. The
Department of North Missouri's primary aim was to
combat guerillas. In 1865, he mustered out as a major
general.

After the war he was assistant commission for the
Freedman's Bureau of Abandoned Lands in Kentucky
and Tennessee. He returned to New York becoming a

successful banker. And in 1874, President U.S. Grant appointed him to the Bureau of Indian Affairs. He ran for President as the candidate of the Prohibition Party. He passed away July 9, 1890

Lt. Col. Erastus Morse (Union)

Little is known of Lt. Col. Morse other than he had a very active part in the Civil War in Central Missouri. He commanded the 10th Missouri Volunteers, and saw extensive action. Most of this was in pursuit of guerillas. In November 1861, he was in pursuit of a band of guerillas under the command of Capt. John Sweeney in Chariton, Howard, and Randolph Counties. Also in November, he arrested H.C. Schwab and Stewart Hatton for bridge burning. In December of 1861, his unit was the first to occupy the University of Missouri. Morse was killed defending the North Missouri Railroad in December of 1861 after much activity in the area protecting Union assets from Confederate guerillas.

Colonel John Poindexter (Confederate)

Colonel John Poindexter Confederate was the son of David and Elizabeth (Watts) Poindexter and was born in Montgomery County, Kentucky on October 12, 1825. He relocated to Randolph County, Missouri and there in 1861 enlisted in the Confederate Army as the captain of a Confederate unit in the Third Division Missouri State Guard. His first action was holding up a train at Allen, Missouri in Randolph County on Aug 28, 1861. He took part in the Battle of Lexington where he was slightly wounded. He then returned to North Central Missouri where he began recruiting.

In January of 1862, he was in command of the Confederate forces at the Battle of Roan's Tan Yard (Silver Creek). Poindexter having only raw recruits the battle resulted in a Union victory. Poindexter was in command of the 4th and 5th Regiments of the Third Division of the Missouri State Guard at the Battle of Pea Ridge.

Poindexter then returned to North Central Missouri where he once again began recruiting. In August of 1862, his unit now called Poindexter's Regiment seized the town of Carrolton with 1200 to 1500 men. Union Colonel Guitar's 9th Missouri Cavalry picked up Poindexter's trail and this began a 250 mile pursuit that lasted only a week. At Little Compton Ferry on the Grand River a running battle began between Poindexter's Regiment and the 9th Calvary Missouri State Militia. Poindexter's men were able to halt the pursuit by burning a bridge across the Muscle Fork of the Chariton River.

On September 1st of 1862, Col. Poindexter was captured in Chariton County. Union commander Brigadier General J. M. Schofield wanted Poindexter executed to serve as an example. Colonel Lewis Merrill selected an execution date, but no order of execution was ever issued. He remained in Myrtle Street Prison in St. Louis until sometime in 1864 when he was exchanged for Union soldiers held prisoner by the Confederate Army. He returned to Randolph County, where he remained until he died on April 14, 1869. He is buried in Antioch Christian Church Cemetery in Eastern Randolph County.

Poindexter was the first Confederate officer tried and sentenced for espionage during the entire war.

Brigadier General Lewis Merrill

Lewis Merrill was born in New Berlin, Pennsylvania on October 28, 1834. He was the son of James and Sarah Merrill. He graduated West Point in 1855. His first assignment was with the First Dragoons and he went on the Utah Expedition

In 1861 he organized Second Missouri Volunteer Cavalry. This unit was commonly called Merrill's horse. Merrill's horse saw extensive action against guerillas in Central Missouri. Some of this activity was in Randolph County, Missouri. By 1864, he was in charge of the cavalry bureau headquartered out of Saint Louis. While serving in that capacity he took part in combat He was then transferred to Georgia and Alabama to fight guerillas.

After the war, he was place in command of the military district in York County, South Carolina with instructions to break up the Ku Klux Klan. Merrill remained there until his retirement in 1886. He passed away ten years later on February 27th in Philadelphia.

Major General W.S. Rosecrans

William Starke Rosecrans was born September 6, 1819 in Delaware County, Ohio to Crandall Rosecrans and Jemima Hopkins. His father was adjutant to General William Henry Harrison during the War of 1812. Rosecrans did not receive much in the way of formal education. Instead, he educated himself for the most part by reading books. At age 13 he took a job as a clerk in Utica. Ohio. Rosecrans decided to try for West Point and was interviewed by Congressman Alexander

Harper. Harper had planned to nominate his own son for West Point, but was so impressed by Rosecrans that he nominated him instead. Rosecrans graduated West Point in 1852 ranking fifth out of 56 cadets. Other members of his class included James Longstreet, Abner Doubleday, D.H. Hill, and Earl Van Dorn. He met Ann Elizabeth Hegeman at his graduation, and they were married in August of 1843.

Rosecrans served in various positions in the Army until 1854 when he resigned and took up mining, and later designing and building lock and dam systems. At the start of the Civil War he volunteered his services to Ohio Governor William Dennison who made him aide-de-camp to Maj. Gen. George B. McClellan. He was promoted to colonel and briefly commanded the 23rd Ohio Infantry regiment, and then was promoted to brigadier general on May 16, 1861,

He took part in the West Virginia Campaign with victories at Rich Mountain and Corrick's Field for which his superior Maj. Gen. McClellan took credit. After McClellan's failure at the First Battle of Bull Run, Rosecrans was placed in command of what was to become the Department of Western Virginia. In 1862, the Department of West Virginia became the Mountain Department, and General John C. Fremont was placed in command. Without a command of his own, Rosecrans was sent to the Western Theater. There he took part in the Battle of Corinth and the Battle of Luka as well as the Second Battle of Corinth.

Rosecrans continued as a fighting general until January of 1864. It was then he was sent to the Department of Missouri, a position he served in until December. While in command of the Department of Missouri, the greatest amount of guerilla activity took part in Central Missouri, and Rosecrans was largely responsible in organizing the Army to fight this activity. Rosecrans resigned from the Army March 28, 1867.

After the war he took an interest in railroads and was one of the organizers of Southern Pacific Railroad. He continued in various business interests and in 1880 was elected as a U.S. Representative for the State of California. He served until 1884. Rosecrans passed away March 11, 1898 in Redondo Beach, California.

Bibliography

Dyer, Frederick, *A Compendium of the War of the Rebellion Compiled and Arranged from Official Records of the Federal and Confederate Armies,* University Publications of America – 1994

Keller, Rudi, *Life During Wartime: 1861: the War Comes to Missouri,* Columbia Daily Tribune Library – 2013.

Keller, Rudi, *Life During Wartime: 1862,* Columbia Daily Tribune Library – 2013.

Nichols, Bruce, *Guerrilla Warfare in Civil War Missouri,* McFarland & Co., Inc., Publishers – 2007

Waller, Alexander H. *History of Randolph County, Missouri,* Bibliolife DBA of Bibilio Bazaar II LLC – *2015*

Williams, Walter, *A History of Northeast Missouri,* Lewis Publishing Company – 1913

History of Randolh and Macon County, St. Louis National Historical Company – 1884